HOPE HANLEY'S

PATTERNS for NEEDLEPOINT

HOPE HANLEY'S
PATTERNS for NEEDLEPOINT

Drawings by Trudy Nicholson
Photographs by Bonnie Boyle

CHARLES SCRIBNER'S SONS
NEW YORK

Library of Congress Cataloging in Publication Data

Hanley, Hope.
    Hope Hanley's Patterns for Needlepoint

    Bibliography: p.109
    1. Needlework—Patterns. I. Title.: Patterns for Needlepoint
TT753.H36   1976   746.4'4   75-25627
ISBN 0-684-14468-9

1 3 5 7 9 11 13 15 17 19 YD/C 20 18 16 14 12 10 8 6 4 2

Printed in the United States of America

*To My Son, Walter
My faithful opinion giver*

ACKNOWLEDGMENTS

Before this book was finished, many people had contributed to its contents and helped me in various ways. My friends Rita Adrosko and Doris Bowman of the Textile Division of the Smithsonian Institution, Washington, D.C., and James O'Neill of the District of Columbia Library gave generously of their time to help me with design sources. Lise Woodard and my daughter, Lee, worked diligently completing canvases for the photographs. Bonnie Boyle and Trudy Nicholson did their usual beautiful work and also helped me keep the details of the book straight. Francoise Woodard boosted me along with her unfailing encouragement. The Elegant Needle and the American Needlework Center, both of Washington, D.C., helped me expand my color palette. Elinor Parker, my editor, displayed unbelievable patience in my delays and excuses. To all these people I am extremely grateful.

Books by Hope Hanley

Needlepoint
New Methods in Needlepoint
Needlepoint in America
Needlepoint Rugs
Fun with Needlepoint
The ABCs of Needlepoint

CONTENTS

FOREWORD

The origin of the word "pattern" is a medieval Latin word, *patronus,* which means "to be imitated." I hope that is just what you will do—imitate, borrow, and adapt the patterns from this book to your own delight and taste. The design ideas were drawn from many sources—books, old samplers, textiles, and museum exhibits. All of the designs were adapted for needlepoint by the author. Three books were used extensively for ideas—those by Archibald H. Christie, Edmund V. Gillon, and Claude Humbert (see the bibliography for titles and publishers). The country of origin and the approximate date of the design are given when known. A few of the designs are original—no source can be given other than the mists of the author's memory.

A great source of inspiration was a family scrapbook compiled by Miss Kate Armstrong in the 1840s in England. It is a collection of needlework samples made by various members of her family. There are penciled captions under the basted-in sample as to which relative's work it was, perhaps Great Aunt Frances Bailey's work or Aunt Marian's. Included are samples of fine hemstitching, crochet, knitted lace, and many samples of Berlin designs and patterns. Some of the Berlin patterns appear here just as they were in the scrapbook. Others have been adapted slightly to conform to the larger mesh canvases used today.

The alphabet patterns were inspired by just about anything—rug patterns, tiles, even men's ties. They provide one with an opportunity to personalize one's work. The letters could be used as a border on a commercial kit canvas or as the pattern itself on a self-designed canvas. The alphabet patterns are very simple—surely you will think of more original ways of using the letters in your design. The alphabet samples were all worked on six-mesh leno canvas, the others were worked on ten-mesh leno. It is recommended that a frame be used with the six-mesh leno. It has a great tendency to bias and therefore is not suggested for use as a rug or wall hanging.

PATTERN

Whether or not a pattern is pleasing depends on several factors. Interest is created by line, continuity, texture, scale, and color. Line means the direction in which the pattern moves—that is, the line the eye follows. Your design line should stay on the canvas. A strong line that leads the eye off the canvas should be stopped by a strong, bold border. Other elements can contribute to the effect created by just one factor. For instance, a repeated diagonal slant from one element in a bright color such as red can give a diagonal slant to a pattern even though the bright red elements are arranged in a straight line. It is the color that accentuates the line.

There are certain textbook ways of arranging pattern elements In the accompanying diagrams, consider each square as a separate pattern element. You can arrange your elements one on top of the other, like letter boxes in a square pattern. If you shove the squares over half a square, you have a brick pattern. Turn it on its end, and the brick pattern is called a half-drop. Turn the whole design on one point and you have a diamond arrangement. Then, of course, there are straight lines of pattern called stripes, which

SQUARES

BRICK

DIAMOND

HALF-DROP

can go in three directions: horizontal, vertical, and diagonal. Further variation can be given to a pattern in any one of the above arrangements by angling the pattern elements in more than one direction. One line of elements could be tipped to the left, in a brick pattern, and the next line to the right.

A similarity of pattern elements tends to pull the design together. A variety of shapes makes the eye travel around out of curiosity, thus giving less continuity to the pattern. Using one or two pattern elements over and over, perhaps upside down or tilted, will give a design more continuity than using many shapes.

Design elements can be accentuated by the use of texture. In the case of needlepoint, texture can be achieved with the use of fancy surface stitches. Such stitches as the Smyrna cross stitch, the brick stitch, or any of the long Florentine-type stitches can be useful for textured effects. A textured background around the pattern elements (worked in half cross stitch) will serve to highlight the smoothness of the pattern elements. Be careful not to use too dark a color with the textured stitches or the texture will not be seen.

Scale (or proportion) is deeply affected by color. Small-scale motifs do best with soft colors; large-scale motifs can carry the bright colors. Your eye must decide if a motif fills the space you want it to. You may have to enlarge or reduce a pattern, depending on the canvas you choose. The same pattern on eighteen-mesh-to-the-inch canvas will appear as a mere dot and on six-mesh canvas a two-inch blob. Count the mesh each motif takes and then mark on your canvas the same number of mesh with dressmaker's chalk. This will give you some idea of proportion before you commit yourself to stitching.

Color in embroidery is usually chosen with regard to where the completed object will be used. However, color must be handled carefully because of its ability to recede and advance. This applies to floors as well as chair seats and pillows. Since dark colors recede, this means that a dark rug will not attract the eye or give a "lift" to the floor. A dark color for a chair seat will make the chair appear lower; a light color will "raise" the seat. If you have several bright colors in a room don't try to include them all in one needlepoint project. Teamed together they will cancel each other out. Feature one bright color for each project, modifying it with softer colors. The softer colors will enhance the bright one and let it have the louder say.

A dark background will cool your most intense colors. If you plan to use very bright pattern colors and want them to stay that way after the background is filled in, use a light background color. To focus attention on your motif use a very bright color with a dark one such as dark blue or green. The contrast between the bright color and the dark one attracts the eye. The background color will have to be neutral.

The eye blends color from a distance. Hence a small black-and-white check will look gray in the distance. If your pattern motif is small, be sure that the colors you choose do not blend to a color you do not want. Decide beforehand which color you want to be the dominant one.

Background colors are just as important as the motif colors. If the background color is too strong, this will be the pattern you will see, not the motifs. The colors must balance so that the background will be part of the pattern too. Artists call the background negative space. They say that the negative space has taken over when the background predominates. The background itself begins to take on shape. Here is where scale and color intertwine again. Make the background work for you by leaving an appropriate amount of space (to *your* eye) between each motif, but at the same time keeping the negative space from taking over by using a complementary enough color. This balance of color and scale must be achieved by the eye. Only your eye can be the judge of what is pleasing to you.

A monochromatic color scheme is not the best choice for a repeat pattern, because it is difficult to achieve enough contrast. Colors that are opposite each other on the color wheel are the most effective for contrast. This is true with a triadic color scheme as well. Using a very pale shade of one of the colors for the background is a way of not having to introduce another color into your scheme. It also guarantees a nice, neutral background color.

An artist's glass will help you considerably in choosing your colors. These glasses, which look like a magnifying glass, do just the opposite. They reduce the image of what you are looking at and are also known as reducing glasses. Artists use them to get perspective on their work without having to move from their seat. Choose your colors and then look at them through an artist's glass. If there are any weak colors in your selection, they will fade out. This will save you from working a canvas and then wishing that you had chosen stronger colors. The glass also will give you better perspective on your motif size and shape. You will find that sometimes a motif will look just great while you are holding it close to work on, but from across the room an entirely different aspect will be seen. Bausch & Lomb manufactures a reducing glass. A very adequate substitute is a pair of binoculars held the wrong way to your eyes. However, anyone watching you may wonder about your sanity.

PRACTICAL POINTERS

This is a mix-and-match book—you choose what pleases you. Combine different time periods and national origins; it is *your* design. The interlocking motifs would make a fine lattice framework for little motifs of your own—perhaps little flowers, or favorite animals, or friends' initials. Some of the color combinations in the color photographs were successful, some were not. You don't have to stick to what is shown. Experiment on your own. This is the fun of embroidery books—you can always think of other ways of handling a motif or other colors to use. The books serve as a springboard for your own originality.

Whether you plan to use several motifs from this book for your complete design or just a border, the first step is still the same. You must find the center of the canvas before you start stitching. Fold the canvas in half. Using a light gray crayon or dressmaker's chalk, mark the center mesh. Fold the canvas in half in the other direction and mark this center mesh. Then mark the center mesh from top to bottom in both directions, using the crayon or chalk. If you find you have a center pair of mesh, run a basting thread between them instead. The thread may be pulled free and out as you work. If you have a prestitched design or an already painted canvas, find what you think is the center of the canvas and draw or stitch out from the edges of the design.

The purpose of finding the center of the canvas is to center your design or your border so that it will look even on the canvas. The threads and markings will help you in counting out the motifs. It is best to work from the center of the canvas when you start stitching. If you are using a repeat motif, find the center of the motif and center it on your canvas. In the case of some of the intertwined designs the center may turn out to be an empty background space. Just count to the nearest edge of the design, then do the same on the canvas, counting from the center of your marked canvas. Mark the canvas with the crayon to indicate where your stitching is to begin. Plan how many times the motif will repeat on your canvas, keeping in mind the ultimate size of the completed canvas.

If you plan to use a border design you must find the center of a single-border motif. Count out how many mesh it takes to make one unit of the border. Space them evenly so that you don't end up with half a unit at the end of each line. If you can't figure out how to turn the corner of a border or if the diagram doesn't show a way, you may just have to stop the border abruptly at each end. A medallion-type motif could be used to fill the space. It is a good idea to work about a half-inch of the background color on the outside of the border. This will allow for the curve of the pillow if it is a knife edge. Otherwise some of the border is apt to be lost. This is a good plan for a box pillow, too, as the upholsterer is apt to nibble into the border, and the cording has a tendency to flop over on it.

Here are some general tips that will help make your canvas as handsome as you expect it to be:

1. If you are not using a fancy stitch, try to use the basket-weave version of the half cross stitch when at all possible, even in tiny spots! This will lessen the bias of the finished canvas and will make blocking that much easier.

2. Try to keep the back of the canvas trimmed of tag ends. This is not tidiness for tidiness's sake. Those little tag ends of wool will travel to the front of the canvas as nearby stitches are worked, thus spoiling the clear colors of your work. Try to trim as you stitch.

3. Don't jump from one spot of a color to another across empty canvas. Finish off the thread each time unless there are some nearby stitches to travel under. The reasoning is the same as for

the above, that the fibers work to the front. And furthermore, you might absentmindedly cut a connecting thread while you are trimming tag ends.

4. Please do remember that *each square* of the graphed patterns represents *one stitch*. Count the squares, not the lines separating them. Each square represents one stitch.

A PORTFOLIO OF PATTERNS

Three colors are needed in order to define the design of the six interlocking squares. A fourth color is needed for the background. To make this motif fill more space without repeating it again, try using the three colors of the motif in progressively larger outside borders. One plain border is shown in the color picture.

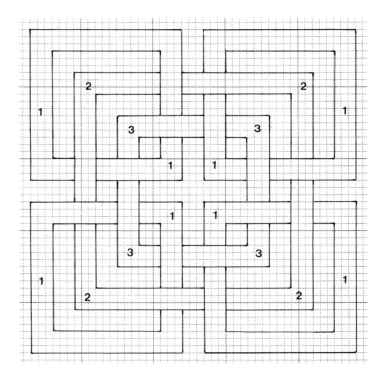

PATTERN 2

This two-color interlocking pattern was adapted from an Egyptian-Roman design of the fourth century. To use it as one super-large design count each square as four squares, thereby enlarging it to four times the original size. It also could be used as a repeat design, separating each unit with three or four rows of mesh.

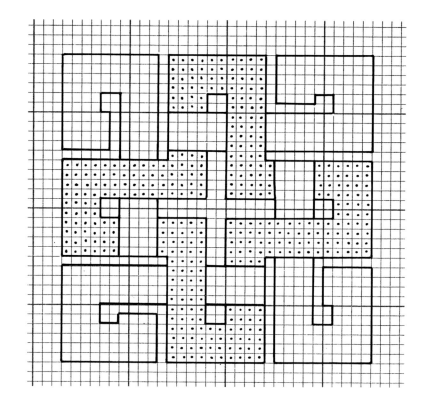

24

The source of this classic-looking interlocked border is probably Greek. It can be used as a border by turning the corners as shown in the diagram, or as an "all-over" stripe. To make the border stand out, try working it in the Smyrna cross stitch or the mosaic stitch. The total number of mesh needed lengthwise for this border must be divisible by ten, with five mesh needed to turn the corner.

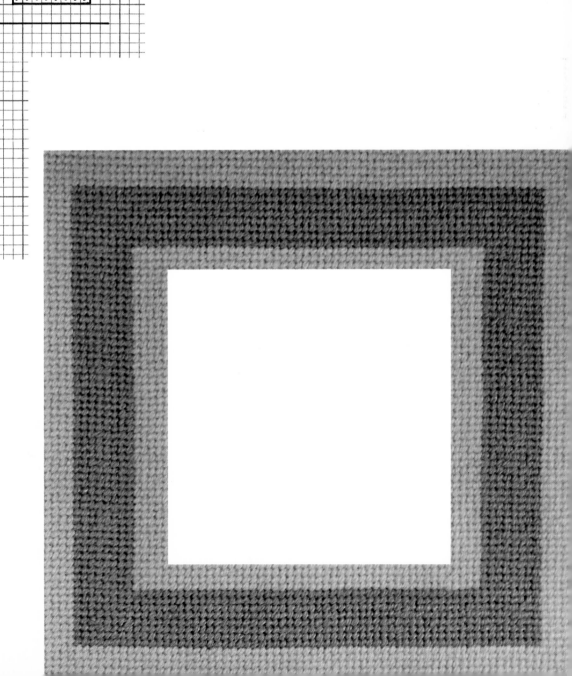

PATTERN 4

In 1598, Jane Bostocke worked a sampler in England that is believed to be the earliest dated example. The three-interlocking-rectangles motif was adapted from her sampler. Three contrasting colors are needed to define its shape, with a fourth color for the background.

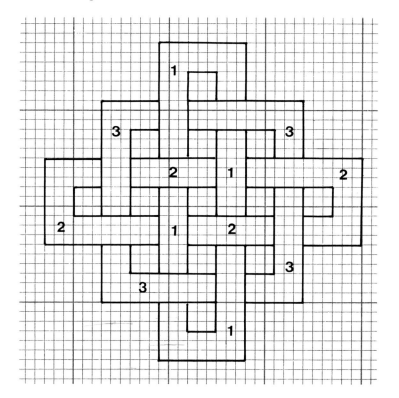

This two-color twist border was found in a late nineteenth-century pattern book from Germany. It is as effective with two fairly close colors as it is with two contrasting colors. The total number of mesh needed lengthwise for this border must be divisible by eight. The number of mesh needed to turn the corner is twelve each way.

PATTERN 5

PATTERN 6 This is the same interlocking rectangle pattern shown in Pattern Four, only here it is slanted diagonally. It was used in seventeenth-century English samplers and embroideries. Three clearly contrasting colors are needed to show it off to its best advantage, plus a fourth color for the background.

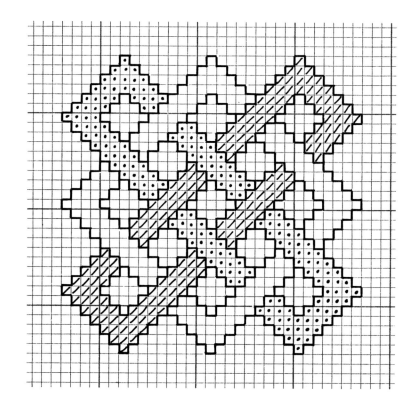

This little interlocking pattern works well as an overall pattern, as a corner medallion, or as a border. When used as a border, it looks best with a few mesh as breathing space between each motif. It was adapted from a seventeenth-century English black-work sampler.

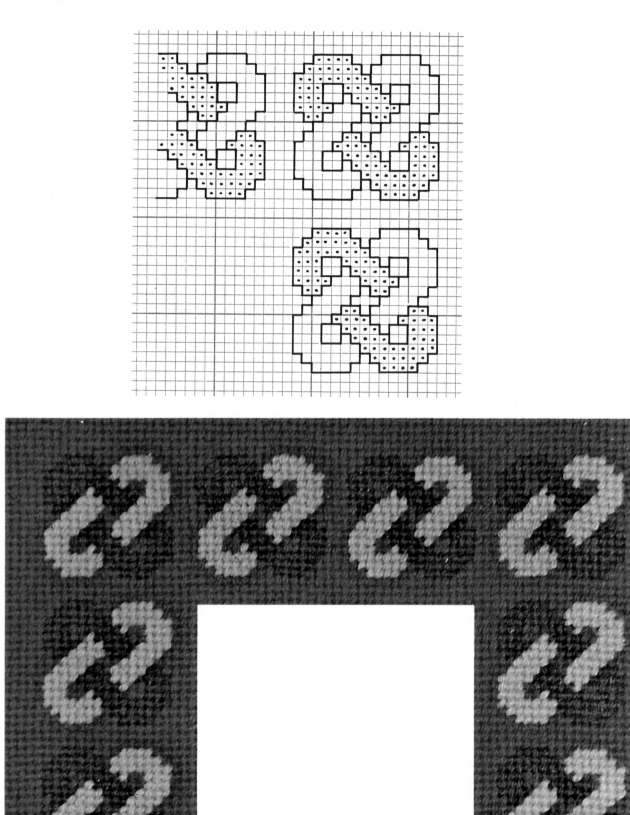

PATTERN 8

The little ribbon medallions need three contrasting colors to show themselves off clearly. As shown in the color photograph, a light and dark shade of the same color will work too, but a color from a different family is needed for the outline.

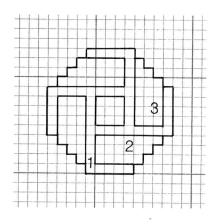

This is another version of the ribbon-twist border. Two contrasting colors are needed to make it really look like ribbon. Each twist requires eight mesh lengthwise. Eleven mesh are needed to turn the corner.

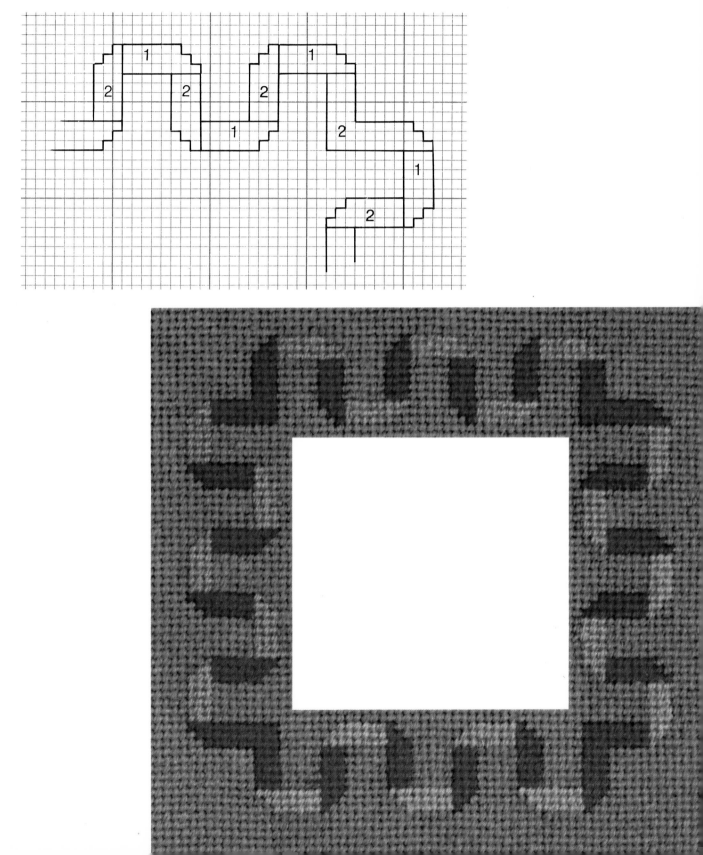

PATTERN 10

Here is another version of a ribbon-type medallion. This one is big enough to be a little border, too. The numbers on the diagram indicate that two colors are needed.

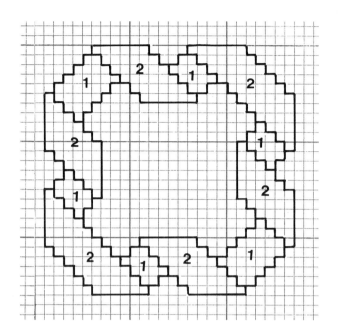

The symbolic chain border is a classic one, probably Greek in origin. Only one color is needed, sharply contrasting with the background color. The length of the repeat measured from the middle of one straight link to the middle of another is twelve mesh. Measuring from the same place on a straight link, eleven mesh are needed to turn the corner.

PATTERN 11

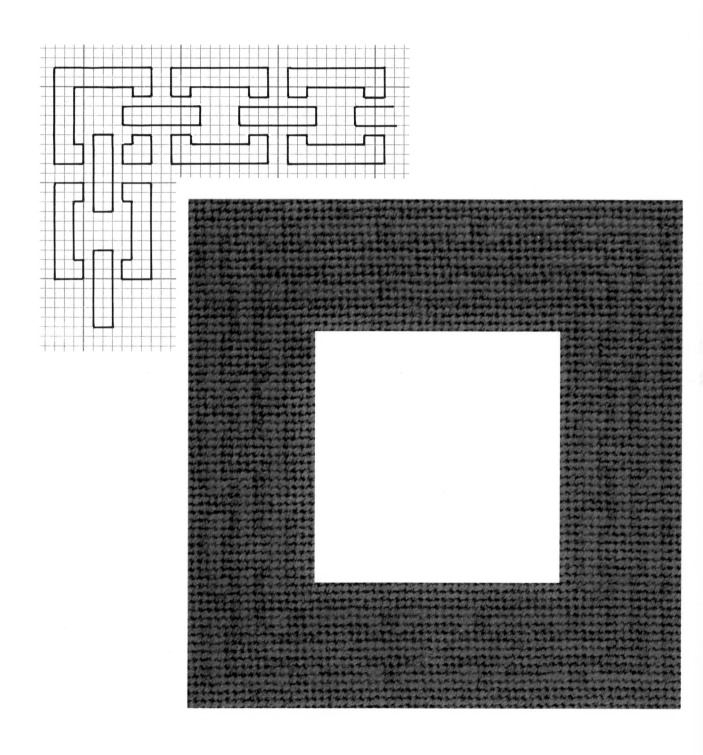

PATTERN 12

This pattern is the same as Pattern Ten except it has been diagramed to be used as a border. Two ways of turning the corners have been shown. This border motif is an old one; the August 1876 *Harper's Bazar* magazine featured it, suggesting it be done in beads for a thermometer and watch stand. The length of the repeat of the pattern is ten mesh per twist. Eight mesh more are needed each way to turn the corner.

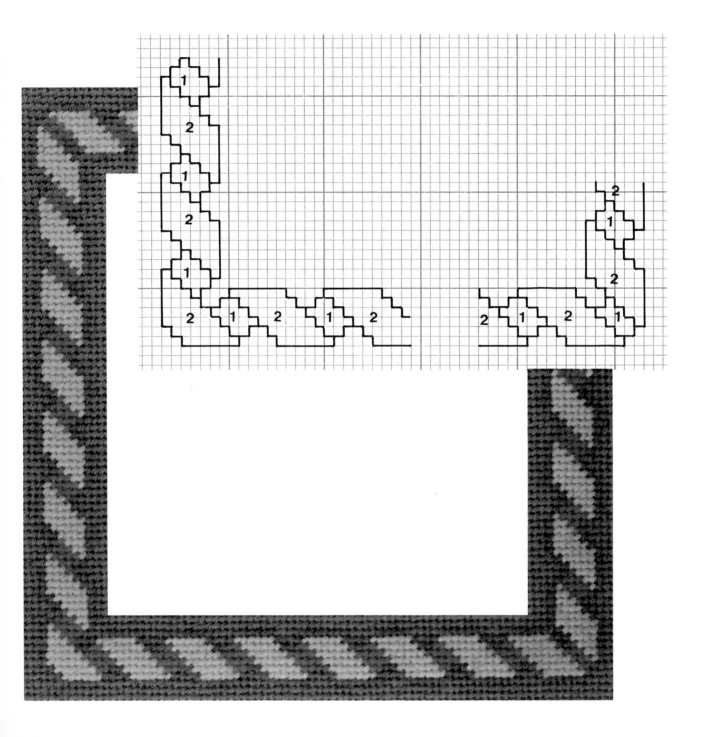

This is a very large and elaborate version of the ribbon-twist border. Since this pattern has dimension or direction, be sure that your center motif does not conflict with it. The length of the repeat is twenty-six mesh, and twenty-six mesh are needed to turn the corner each way.

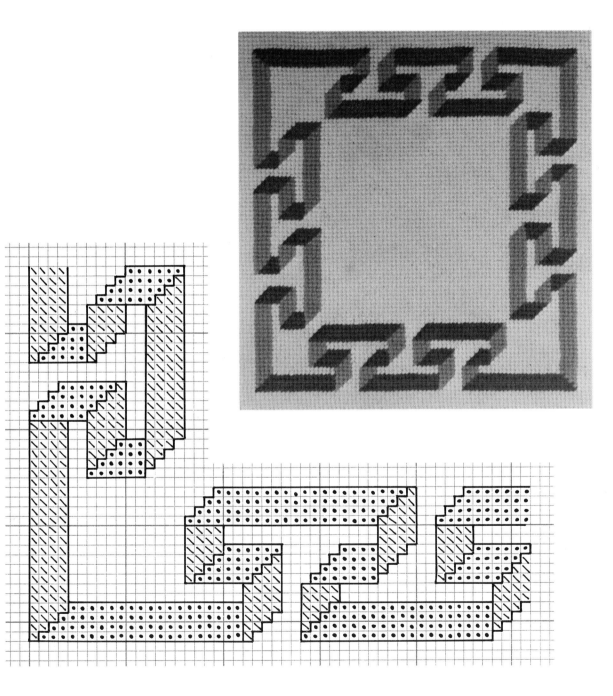

PATTERN 14

The origin of this simple little link border is an 1876 American sampler. Two contrasting colors are desirable to show off the links. Only nine mesh per link are needed (counting from the one background mesh where the links twine). Eleven mesh are needed for the corner link.

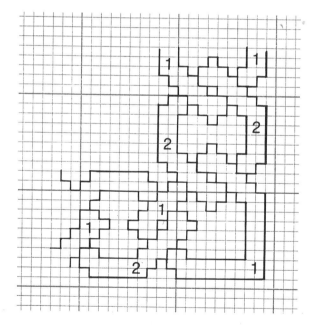

Here is another twist border but with a link added over each twist. **PATTERN**
Three quite contrasting colors are needed to show it off. Nineteen **15**
mesh are needed from the center of one link to the next one. Fourteen mesh are needed to turn the corner each way.

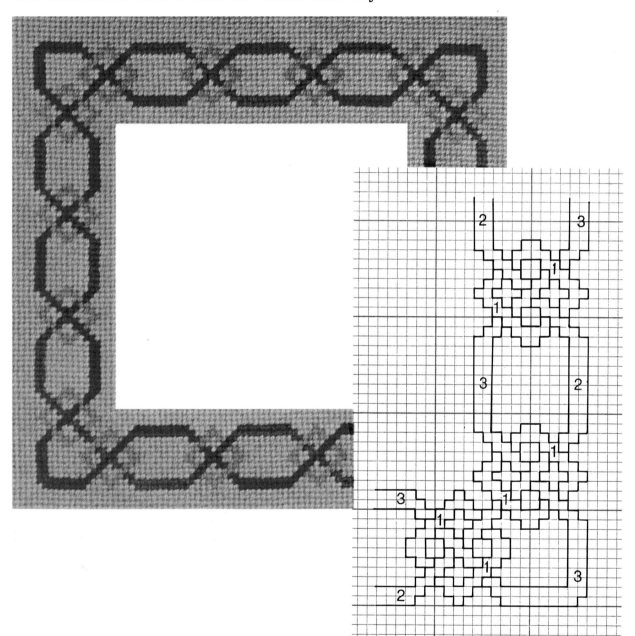

PATTERN 16

The border is a classic Greek one. The easiest way to count the length of a repeat is to count from the middle of one **T**, through a complete one, to the middle of the next one. Thus you have twelve mesh per fret. Only six mesh are needed to complete a corner turn.

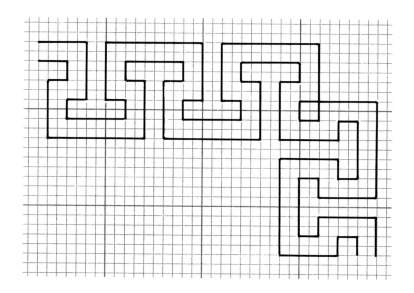

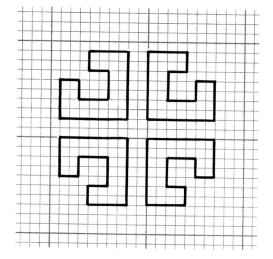

The **S**-like pattern was adapted from a foot-muff border shown in the January 1878 *Harper's Bazar* magazine. The length of each unit of this pattern is thirty-two mesh, plus two more in between to separate them. Only eight mesh are needed to turn the corners.

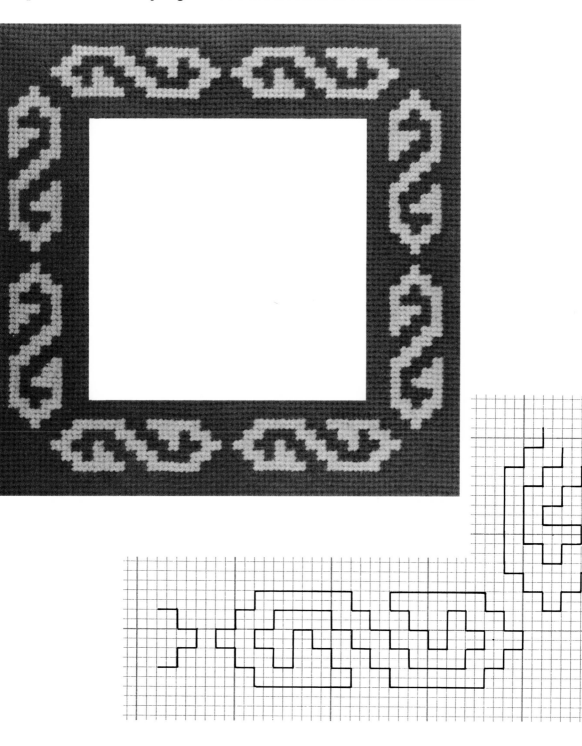

PATTERN 18

This ornate border pattern was adapted from a late nineteenth-century crochet pattern. Taking a clue from its origin, try working the pattern in a light color against a dark background. Each motif requires thirty-three mesh lengthwise, plus one to separate them. The corner medallion takes fifteen mesh, plus one on each side to separate.

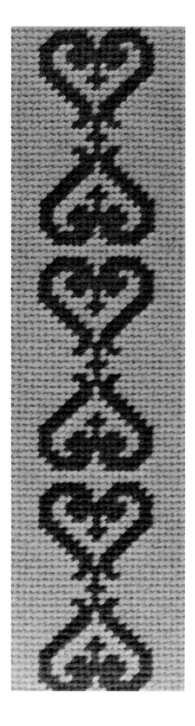

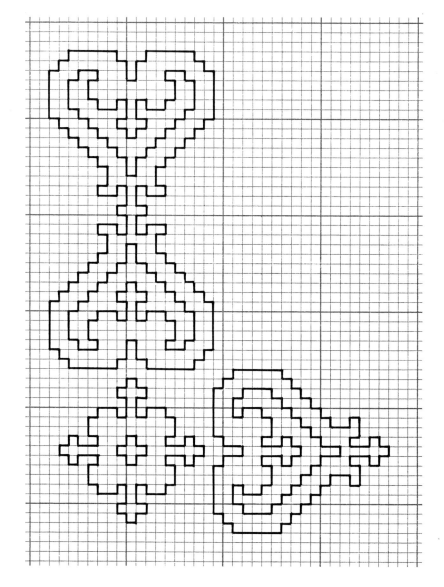

A nineteenth-century crochet pattern was the source of this border pattern too. The length of each **S** is twenty mesh; the connecting bar is two mesh. In counting out your border you will always need one more **S** than connecting bar. Ten mesh are needed for the corner medallions with a mesh on each side to separate them.

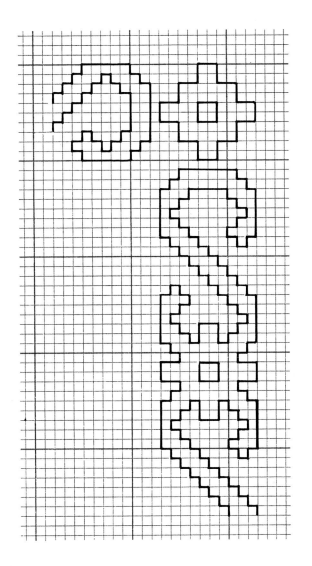

PATTERN 20
An 1877 issue of *Harper's Bazar* magazine included this pattern as a border for a basket. It was to be worked in zephyr wool and filling silk. DMC cotton might do as a latter-day substitute. The pattern has a twenty-six-mesh repeat. Eleven mesh are needed to turn the corners.

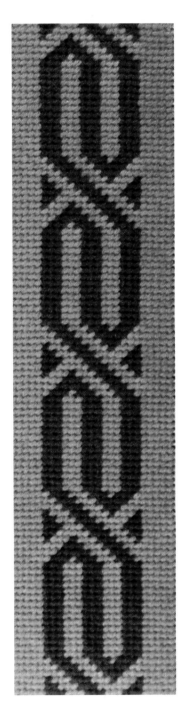

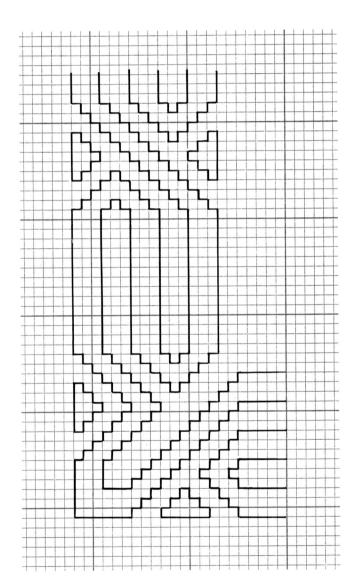

The four-interlaced-hearts pattern may be used as a repeat pattern or as a single medallion. The two (or four) colors must contrast sufficiently or the effect of the pattern will be lost.

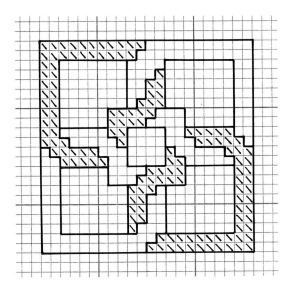

PATTERN 22 This pattern is not a border as much as it is fancy corners for a plain band border. It would look well bordering a monogram or some other small and sentimental motif. The motifs look lost if they are set too far apart from each other.

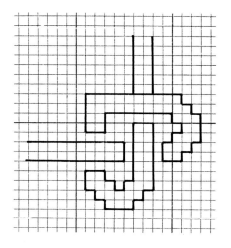

The source of this border is an Italian lace book published in 1531. The knotted hearts of this octagonal border may be spread farther apart than they are in the accompanying diagram. If they are placed too far apart they tend to look skimpy, however. For a small octagonal pillow it makes a very sweet border.

PATTERN 23

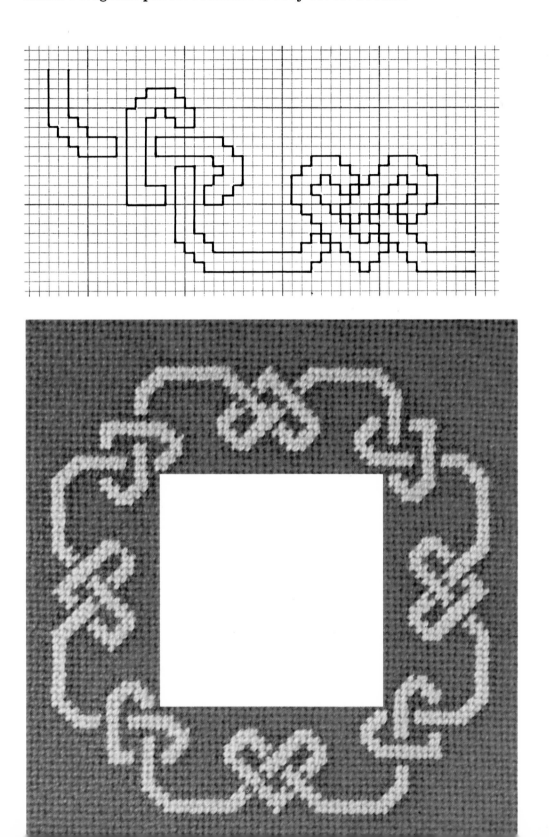

PATTERN 24

The double-wave border was adapted from a Transylvanian rug border. It can be used as a repeating stripe or as a border. To turn the corner for the border, count out three mesh from the base of your last upright wave and start working down at a forty-five-degree angle on the first upright wave of the new row. The length of the repeat for the border is twenty-four mesh. Seven mesh more in both directions are needed to turn the corner.

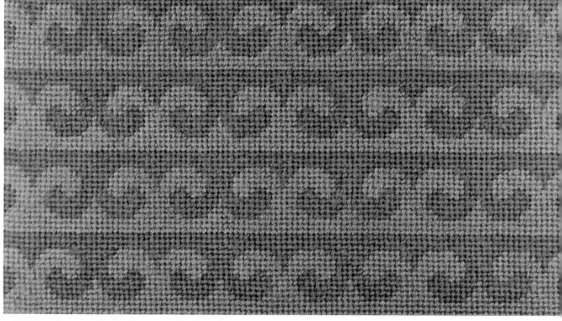

46

This stripey pattern was adapted from a Shiraz Kelim rug motif. Over a large area it becomes rather tedious to work. It could also be used as a border by mitering the corner to make it fit.

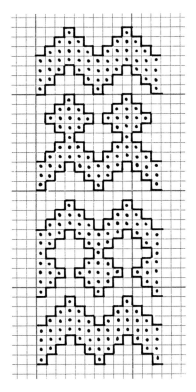

PATTERN 26 The bush-and-candlestick pattern was taken from a piece of Coptic textile at the Smithsonian Institution in Washington, D.C. The pattern dates from sometime before the tenth century. The length of the repeat on this pattern is an exceptionally long one—fifty-eight mesh. This accounts for two candlesticks and bushes, plus four mesh at one end to separate them from the next set.

Since the eight-pointed star is so large, it can carry very bright colors. Please note that if you want to enlarge or shrink the space between the motifs, the number of mesh between the stars horizontally and vertically always will be different. As diagramed here, the stars are six mesh apart horizontally and eight mesh apart vertically.

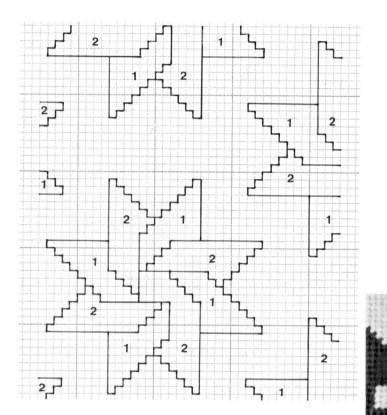

PATTERN 28

The Armstrong scrapbook was the source of this pattern. The Scotch stitch is used for the squares tucked in the corners of the Byzantine stitch "stairs." The Scotch stitch is worked in the opposite direction from the slant of the Byzantine stitch to help combat any bias that might be created by all the slanted stitches. Good, clear, contrasting colors are needed to make this pattern effective.

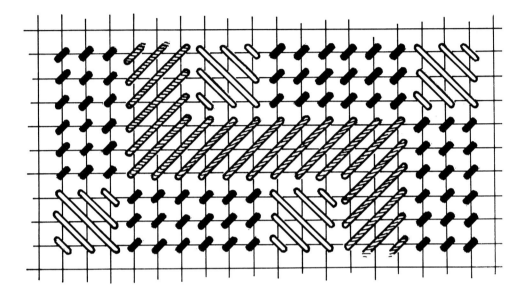

This eye-popping pattern was inspired by illustrations in a book on optical art by René Parola (see the bibliography). It should be worked in cross stitch in order to make the lines of the pattern connect with each other when they switch direction. Only half the pattern has been given here, since it repeats itself. Start working in one corner and when half the canvas is completed, turn the pattern around. Start in the corner diagonally opposite the one you previously started in.

PATTERN 29

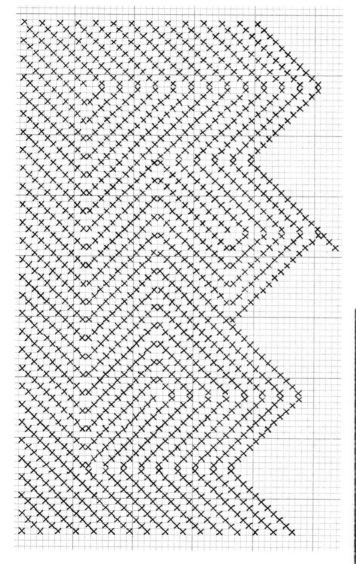

PATTERN 30 The rows-of-hearts pattern is reminiscent of a bargello pattern but actually was adapted from an 1877 tidy border shown in the *Harper's Bazar* magazine. This pattern could be changed into a border pattern by working one row of hearts as shown in the diagram with one mesh separating the hearts. Then turn the canvas upside down and work another row of hearts in another color, fitting the points of one row into the space in between the hearts of the previous row.

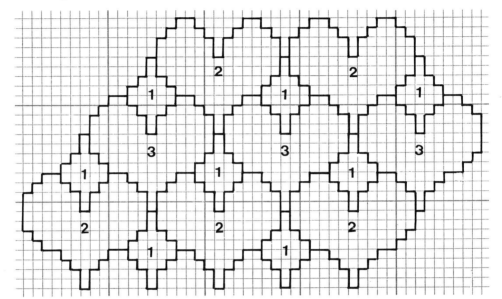

The little two-by-two mesh centers of this pattern have been worked in the Smyrna cross stitch. The fact that they are all the same color gives the pattern continuity. The pattern was adapted from the Kate Armstrong scrapbook. Five different colors are needed.

PATTERN 32

This pattern seems to have a Near Eastern flavor but is a favorite all over the world. Since it is rather large, striking colors could be used. To add texture one color could be worked in the half cross stitch and the other in the Smyrna cross stitch or in the mosaic stitch.

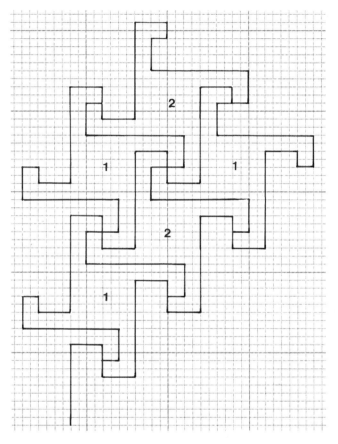

The six-pointed-star pattern was adapted from the background of a Persian miniature. In very soft colors it might serve as a damask-like background for a figurative canvas.

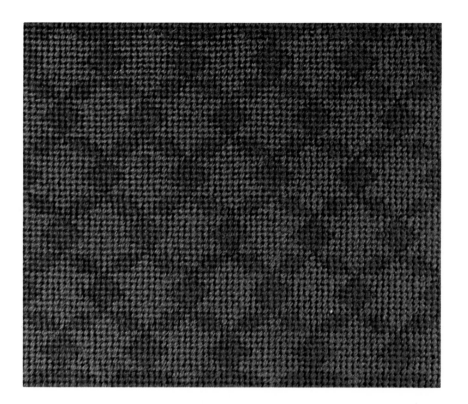

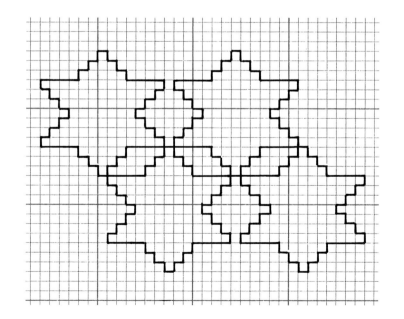

PATTERN 34

A thirteenth-century tile motif was the source of inspiration for this pattern. The color balance of this pattern must be just so or the pattern does not look right. Make sure that the squares in the centers and the starlike shapes are a noncommittal color or these parts will dominate the pattern.

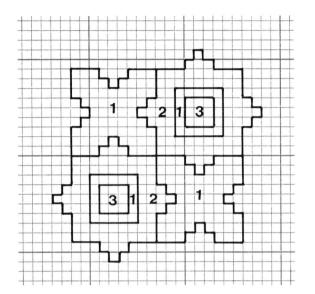

The three-dimensional-letter-box pattern may look quite modern, but it was adapted from a pattern shown in a *Peterson's* magazine of February 1861. A monochromatic color scheme shows off the box effect to the best advantage.

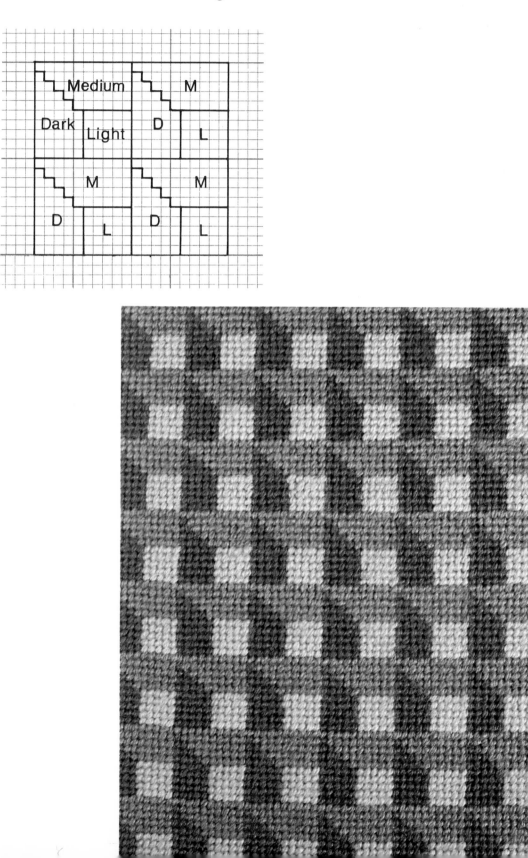

PATTERN 36

To see the three-dimensional quality of the typewriter-key pattern, a monochromatic color scheme is almost a necessity. The faces of the keys were worked in the knit or kalem stitch; the basket-weave stitch would, of course, do as well.

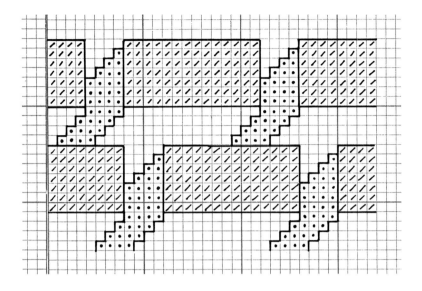

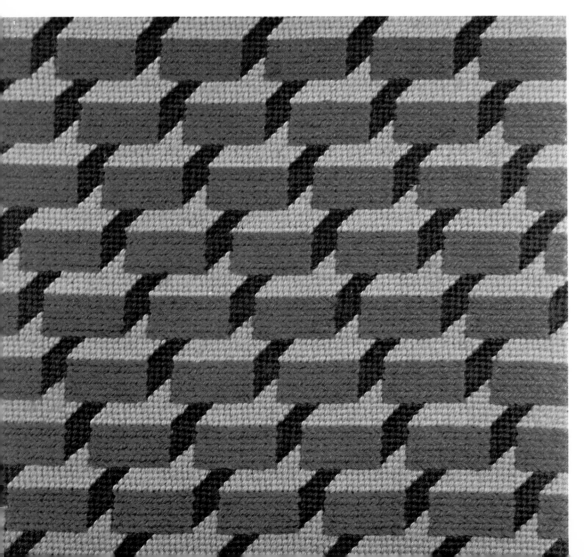

Two sharply contrasting colors are most effective in carrying out this classic pattern. It may be used by itself, or, if two very bland colors are used, it might enliven great expanses of dull background. For this, two analogous colors or two monochromatic colors should be used.

PATTERN 37

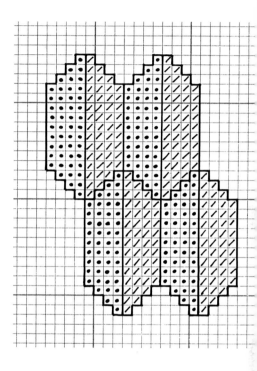

PATTERN 38

A monochromatic color scheme is the most effective one for this three-dimensional pattern. Although the pattern is small, soft colors should be avoided if the pattern is to be seen at all. The square fronts of the little blocks may be worked in basket-weave or in mosaic stitch as shown here. They should be worked in the darkest color.

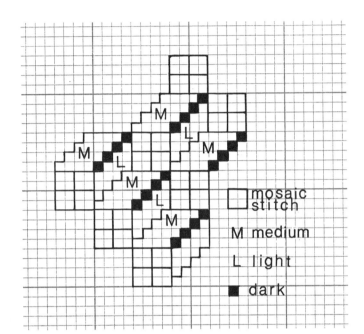

☐ mosaic stitch

M medium

L light

■ dark

This pattern was rather freely adapted from a nineteenth-century Indian cotton-printer's block. All the little dumbbells may be worked in one color if you like or in two colors as shown in the color photograph.

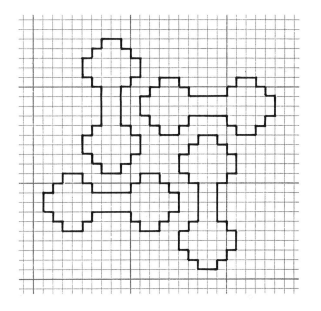

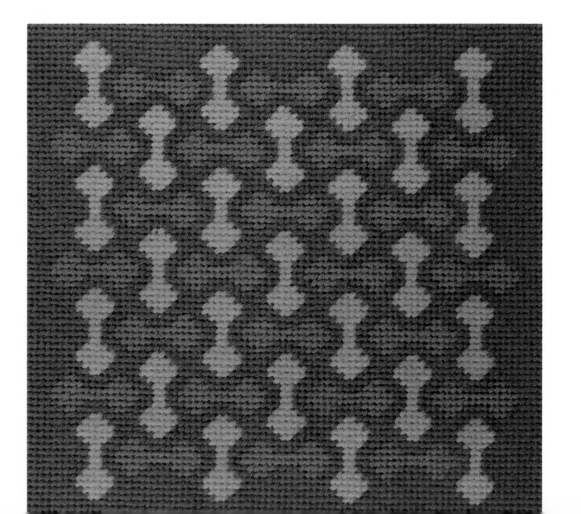

PATTERN 40

By using a dark background color, attention is drawn to the pattern the background creates. A case in point is the double-arrow motif (please excuse the pun). The pattern was adapted from a sixteenth-century Turkish dish.

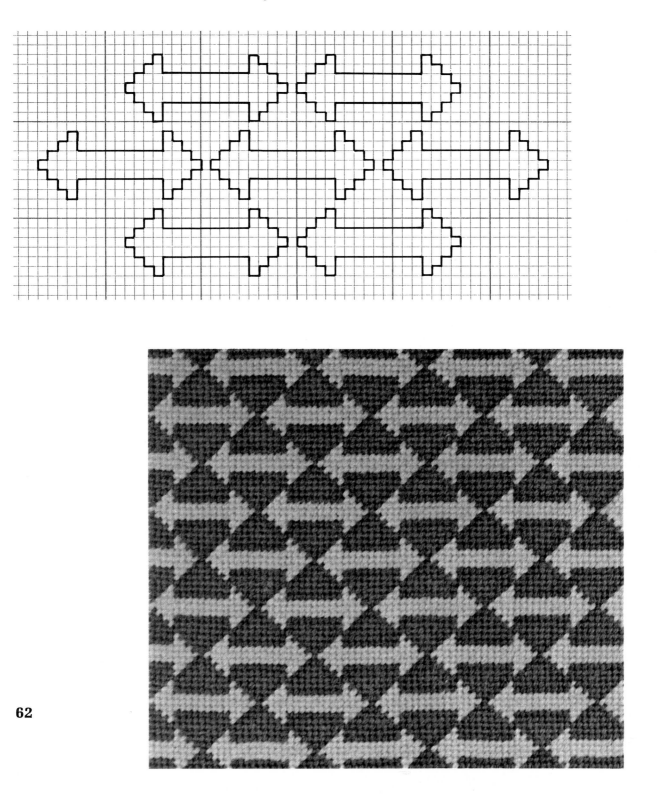

The pinwheel pattern was adapted from a sixteenth-century East Indian motif. At least one bright color is needed to make the pattern stand out, or if you prefer, the background.

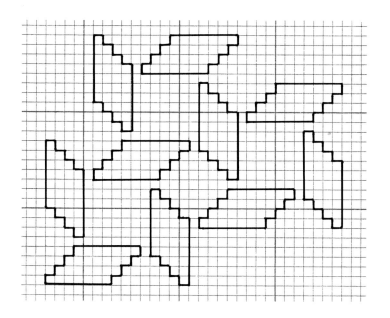

PATTERN 42

Because this pattern is fairly large, strong colors may be used. Use the brightest ones for the **X** shapes; otherwise the background diamonds will shine through as the most important feature of the pattern. Three colors are needed in all.

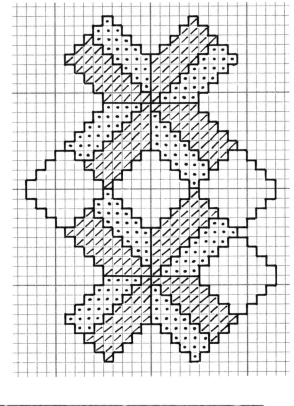

The Armstrong scrapbook yielded this delicate variation on a familiar theme. Four colors are needed where ordinarily two would suffice. The shades in pairs should be very close together to give the smoky effect. The pattern itself need not be as simple as this one. It serves only as a vehicle to show off the smoke bargello.

PATTERN 43

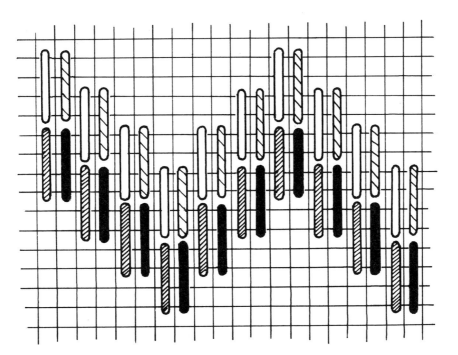

PATTERN 44 This tiny bargello square pattern was a great favorite of the Victorians. It was often worked in a wild mixture of colors rather than the monochromatic scheme favored today. This version was found in the Armstrong scrapbook. Four colors are needed. Rather than finish off the thread for the little center square, weave your needle through the backs of nearby stitches to the next little square. By working the pattern a row of squares at a time, it is easier to keep the color sequence straight, rather than working all of one color at once as some people prefer to do.

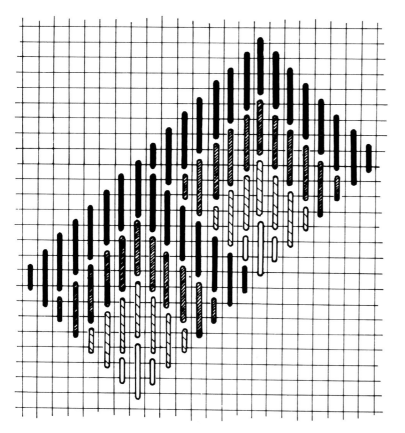

This showy pattern came from a Czechoslovakian sampler of the mid-nineteenth century. In the original it was worked in cross stitch and beads. A splashy array of colors may be used, or a more subtle monochromatic scheme with white as an accent.

PATTERN
45

PATTERN 46

An Elizabethan sweet bag was the source of this double-twisting interlocking pattern. On the original what appear to be primroses fill the large blank spaces. Two contrasting colors are needed for the twists to define them.

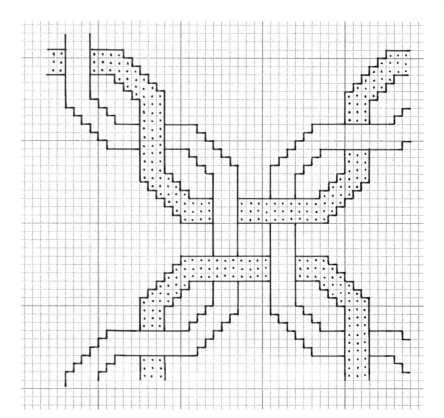

Jane Bostocke's sampler of 1598, believed to be the earliest signed sampler, was the source of the three-color intertwined pattern. This pattern is rather busy and looks best by itself—that is, without motifs in the blank centers. With this pattern it is important that the three colors chosen for the intertwines in this pattern really stand out from the background color.

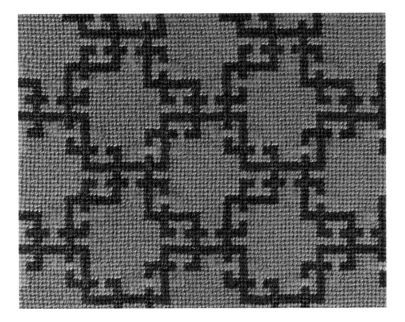

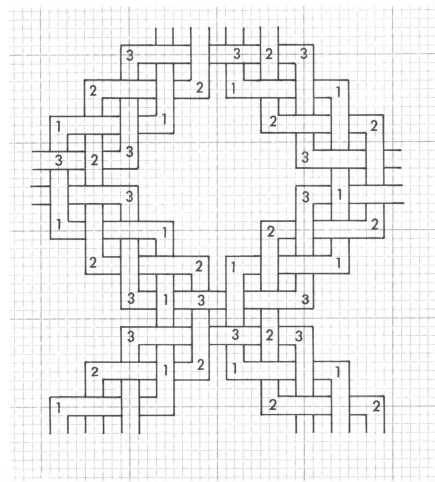

PATTERN 48

This interlocking pattern was also adapted from a seventeenth-century English sampler. The two colors used for the pattern should not be of the same value or they will cancel each other out—for instance, bright orange and bright yellow. The pattern is most striking if a light background color is used.

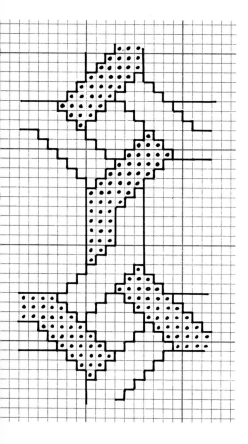

70

This interlocking square pattern looks a lot more complicated than it is. It was adapted from an English sampler of the seventeenth century. Don't worry too much about colors with this pattern. Even if they cancel each other out, the general silhouette of the pattern is still an interesting one.

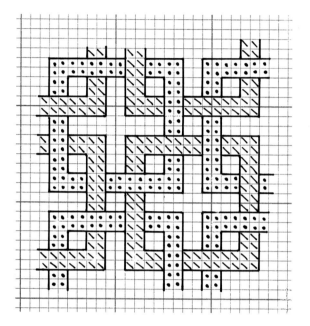

PATTERN 50 This pattern is almost the same as Pattern Forty-nine; it just is set diagonally. Be careful that the background color is not too strong or it will overpower the pattern and all you will see will be the **X**'s and dots of the background.

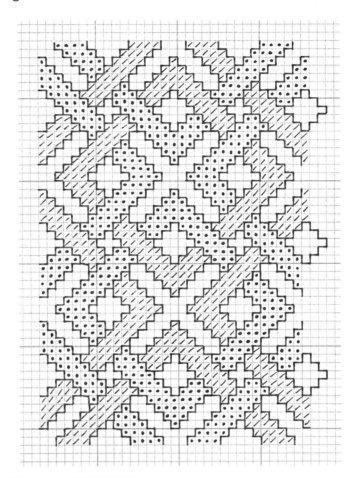

The very elaborate interlaced ribbon pattern was adapted from a seventeenth-century English sampler design. A contrast of colors is not too important for the ribbons, because the pattern itself is interesting enough in outline.

PATTERN 52

This chain-link-fence-like pattern was simplified from a Coptic textile motif from Egypt. A great contrast is not necessary for the chain linking because the design can stand by itself without the aid of color.

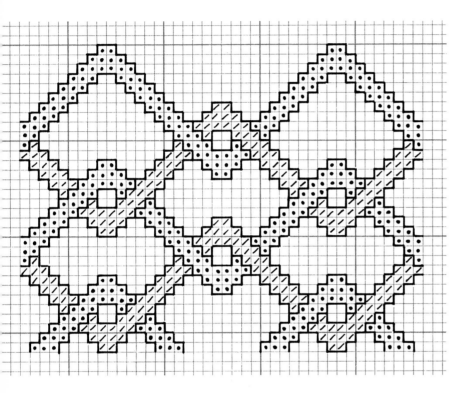

74

This checkered pattern was adapted from an Italian silk damask pattern of the sixteenth century. If you are not careful with the background color choice for this pattern you are apt to end up with it dominating the pattern. Pick one that is paler than the checkered pattern.

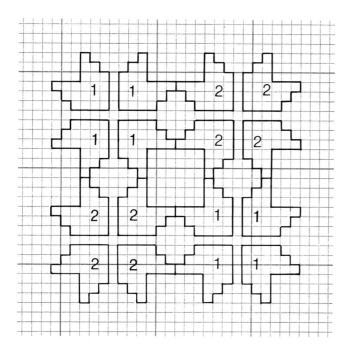

PATTERN 54 Two colors plus a background color are needed for the nested **A** pattern. The contrast should be fairly sharp or the letter will not stand out. To use as a border, work a single horizontal band of the nested **A**'s. Turn the corner by stopping the pattern at the end of one letter, and then leave just a few mesh empty of pattern before starting again at a forty-five-degree angle.

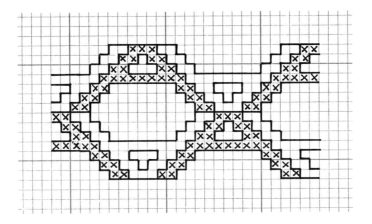

The **B** pattern is meant to be used as a border or as stripes across the canvas. Two colors plus a background color are needed. The letters and the background are designed to be worked in the brick stitch. Directions for the brick stitch are to be found in the stitch dictionary (page 104). If the pattern is used in stripes, separate them with a row of long-armed cross stitches. This pattern is not very amenable to turning corners. It probably would be best to place a square medallion of some sort in the corners rather than trying to match two directions of brick stitch and the ensuing blank spot. Ten mesh plus two separate the letters; twelve in all are needed for each letter **B**.

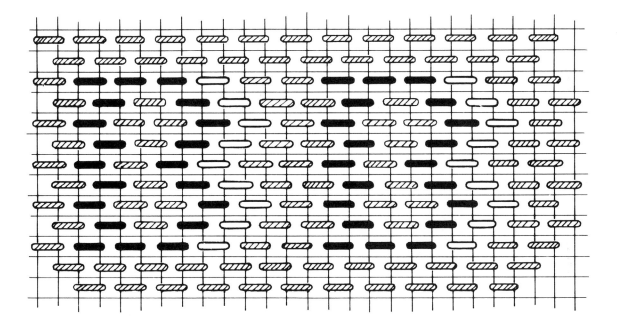

PATTERN 56

The interlocked **C** pattern border has a faintly Victorian look. It is meant to be worked in the half cross stitch except for the little seriflike stitches. They should be worked in cross stitch to guarantee that they stay hooked to the body of the letter. When a line slants from right to left with the half cross stitch, a single stitch will look detached from the rest unless it is worked in cross stitch. Twelve mesh is the length of the repeat for this border. However, it should be counted out carefully, as the spine of the **C** is an uneven number. The corner can be turned in seven mesh each way.

Two colors plus a background color are needed for the letter **D** pattern. The most dominant of them should be placed to the left. This will ensure the viewer's understanding of what letter is meant. The length of one set of **D**'s is eighteen mesh with one mesh in between. Only seven mesh each way are needed for the corner.

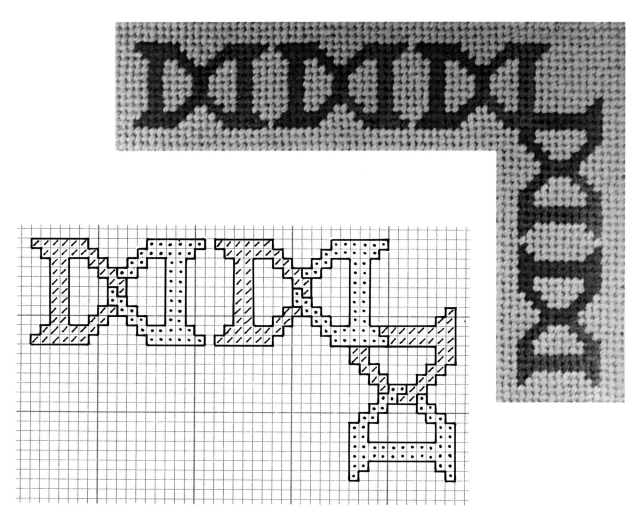

PATTERN 58 The letter **E** may be worked in the half cross stitch, but using a textured stitch will give it more definition. The Smyrna cross stitch is shown in the color photograph. The mosaic stitch would be appropriate, too. The diagrams of these stitches can be found in the stitch dictionary (pages 103-107). The length of the repeat is twelve mesh, with six mesh needed each way to turn the corner.

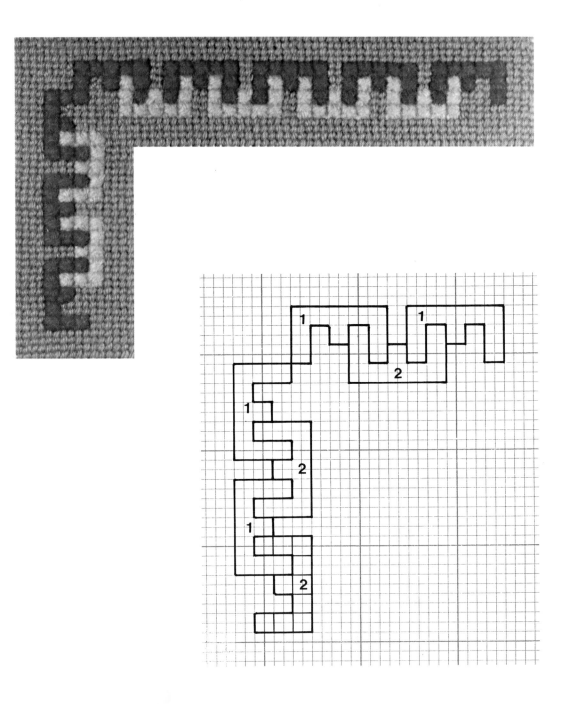

The pattern for the letter **F** medallion was adapted from a sixteenth-century Mogul pattern. Only one color plus the background color is needed. However, if the mesh between the **F**'s were eliminated, you could use two colors for the letters opposite each other. This would make a smaller, tighter design.

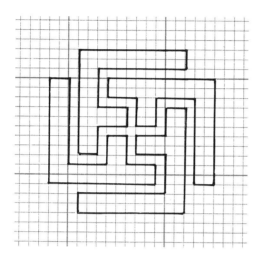

PATTERN 60

There are not too many ways to arrange the letter **G** into a pattern and still have it look even slightly like the letter it is supposed to be. The pattern as given also could be closed up with no background space around it, thus making it an overall pattern. If used this way it would be well to choose at least four colors for the letter and a fifth for the background.

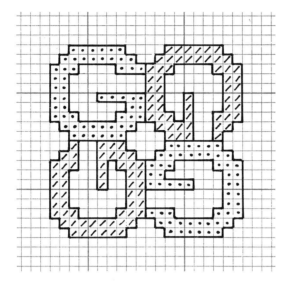

82

This pattern can be reduced to two rows of the letter or could be enlarged to several rows. To make the letter look more like an **H** add a four-mesh square to each end of the two uprights. At least three colors of equal intensity are needed for the letters, with a milder color for the background. Each letter is eight mesh wide. Count your space for the outside row. Six mesh are needed to turn the corners each way.

PATTERN
61

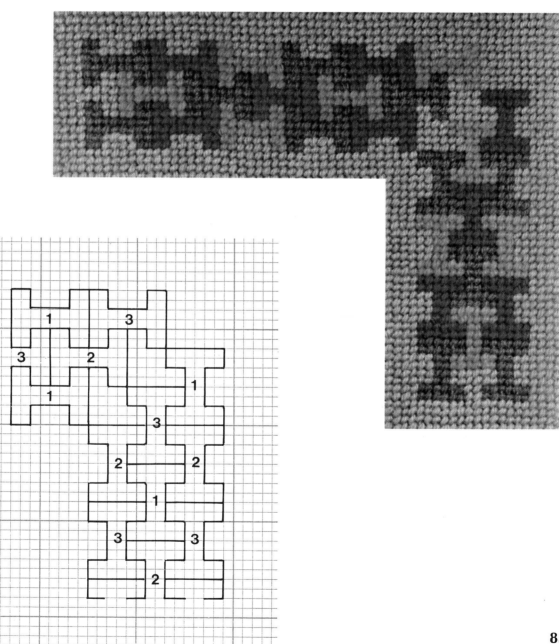

PATTERN 62

As a border this letter is quite interesting; as an overall pattern it becomes a bit of a bore. It can be worked all in half cross stitch or as shown in the illustration in the mosaic stitch. Another variation would be to work the letter itself in the half cross stitch and the dots in the Smyrna cross stitch. Each letter unit is four mesh wide. Count on eight mesh each way for the corner.

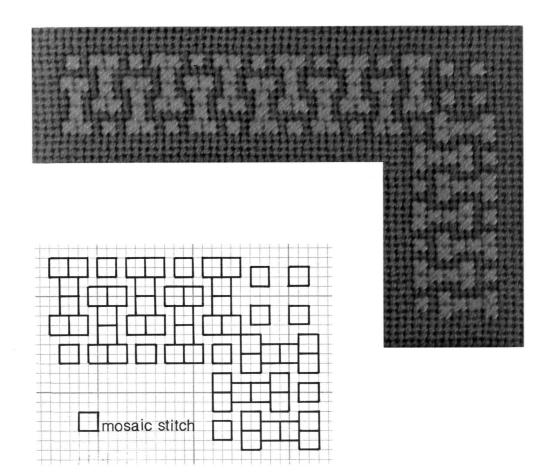

☐ mosaic stitch

The letter **J** needs the serif at the top in this pattern arrangement; otherwise it looks like a nice collection of fishhooks. Only two colors are needed for this pattern, one for the letter and one for the background.

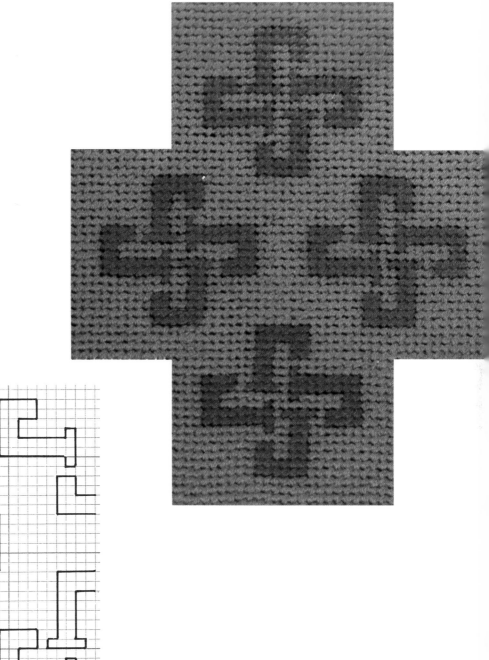

PATTERN 64

The **K** pattern has, for some reason or other, a very African flavor. It is a very strong pattern. Two colors are needed for the letters, and another for the background.

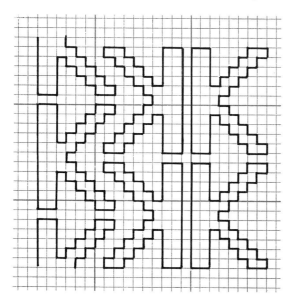

The **L** pattern should be handled in units of two, thus forming little bricks. In units of two it is easier to turn corners so that all the **L**'s are pointing in a consistent direction. All definition of the letter as an **L** is lost if it is used as an overall pattern. The centers of the letter can be worked in half cross stitch or as shown in the mosaic or the Smyrna cross stitch. Each brick unit of two **L**'s is eighteen mesh long. Count twelve mesh to turn the corner.

PATTERN
65

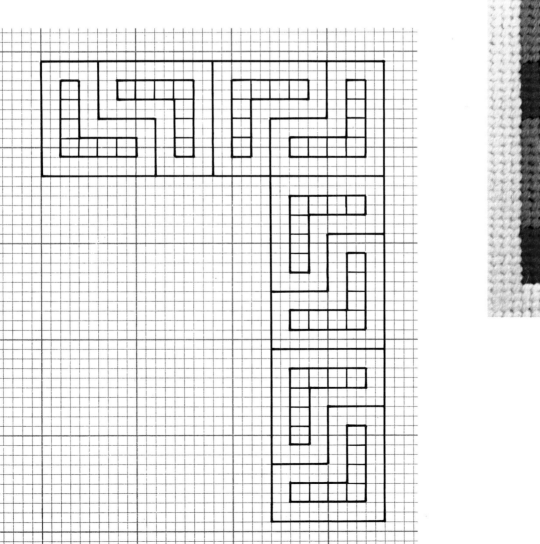

PATTERN 66

Two nicely balanced colors are needed to show off the **W** pattern; another is needed for the background. If you prefer, call this an **M** pattern. Seventeen mesh are needed for each letter on the outside row with seven mesh in between. Only four mesh in each direction are needed to turn the corner.

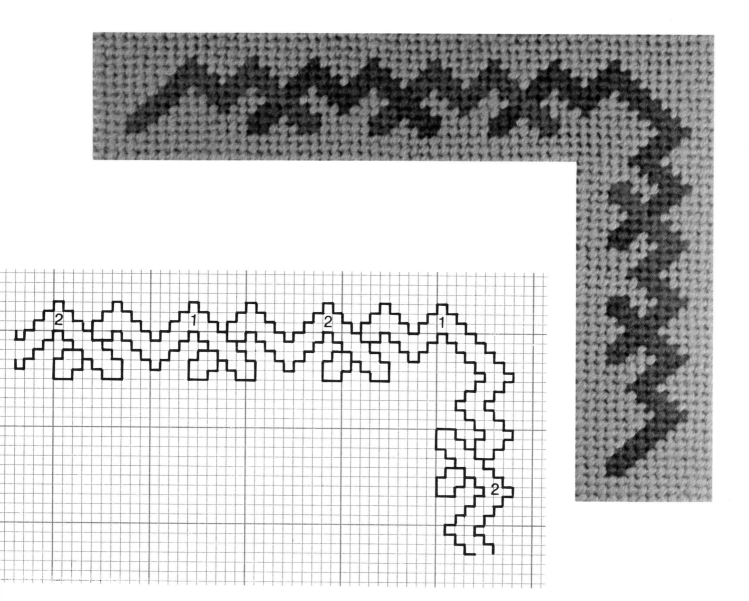

The pattern for the **N** border was adapted from a pre-Columbian Peruvian design. Fourteen mesh are needed for each letter. Eighteen mesh are needed to turn the corner from one direction, but only sixteen mesh from the other direction. This, you will notice, is because of the long stroke coming from the other row. Two colors are needed for this border, one for the letters and one for the background.

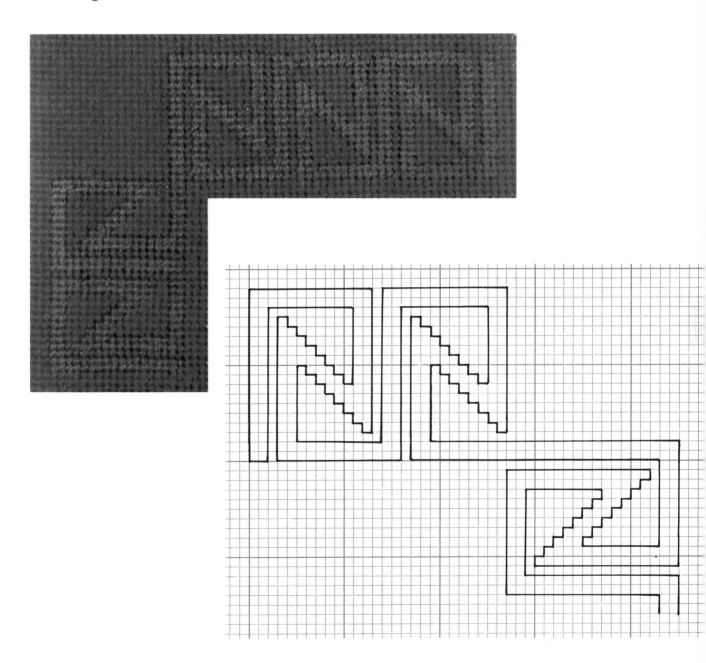

PATTERN 68

The linked **O**'s take two colors to show their pattern, plus another color for the background. The repeat of the border is eight mesh long, counted from the middle of the linkage. It takes sixteen mesh coming from one direction to turn the corner and fifteen mesh coming from the other direction. This is again counted from the middle of the linkage.

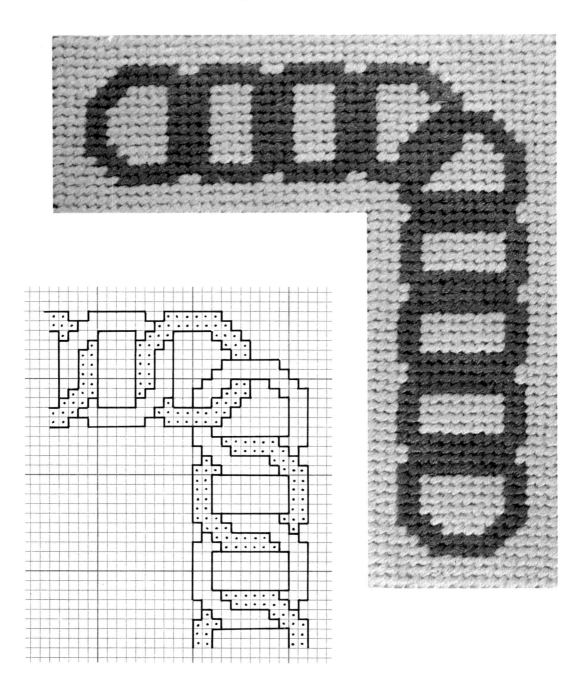

The pattern for the letter **P** was adapted from a seventeenth-century English sampler. The element that gives it definition is the use of another color on the outside outline. Use two bright colors to show off the letter and another for the background.

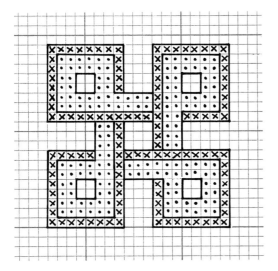

PATTERN 70 The **Q** pattern also needs two bright colors to make it show off to the best advantage. A blander color is needed for the background. Each letter repeat is eleven mesh long with one mesh in between. Eight mesh are required to turn the corner in each direction.

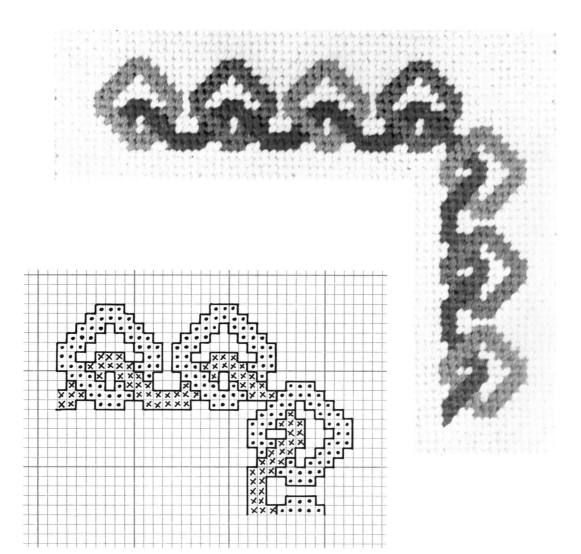

The grouped **R**'s make a bold pattern with the background space **PATTERN** making a pattern of its own. Two colors are needed for the letters, **71** another for the background.

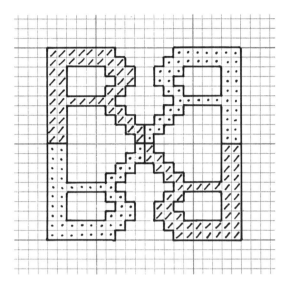

PATTERN 72

This pattern was adapted from an age-old Oriental rug motif. Though it may not be too discernible in the photograph, two different shades of red were used. One shade was used for the **S**'s and another for the honeycomb frame. Using two closely related colors this way adds a certain liveliness to the pattern. The pattern could be worked in the half cross stitch instead of the brick stitch as shown here.

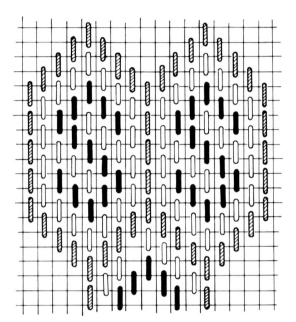

The pinwheel **T**'s require two colors of equal value to make the pattern balance evenly. A third color is needed for the background. If the **T**'s are enlarged to make a bigger pattern, too much background space is created. When this happens the tightness of the pattern is lost.

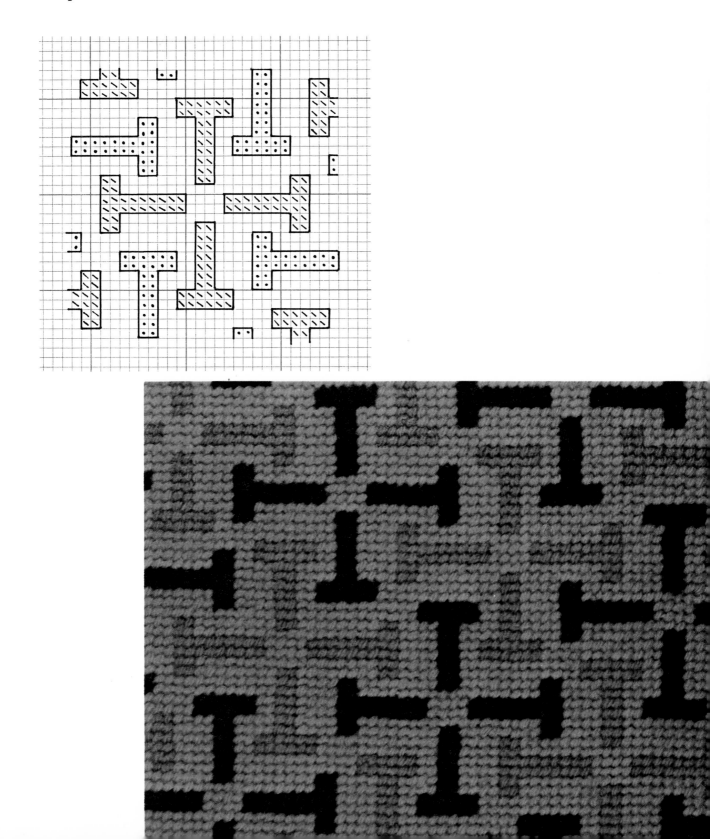

PATTERN 74 This pattern will work as a border as well as an overall pattern. It is rather hard to turn a corner gracefully with it. It is best just to stop in the middle of a coil and then start again around the corner. From the middle of one color **U** to the middle of the next **U** of the same color there are eight mesh. Two colors of equal value are needed for the letters; another color is needed for the background.

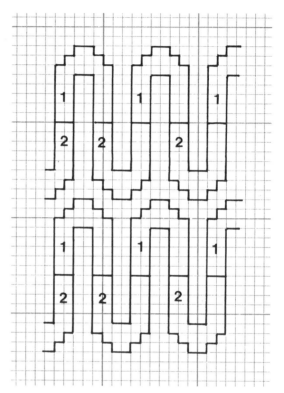

It is hard to do anything very interesting with the letter **V** and still have it retain its **V** look. It has a tendency to look like tire treads or cut-up rickrack no matter what you do. Two colors are needed for the letters in this pattern (brighter than the ones shown in the color photograph, incidentally); another is needed for the background.

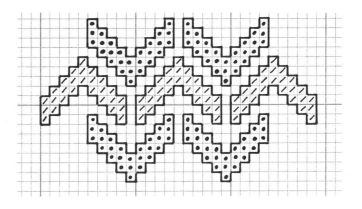

PATTERN 76

It is difficult to tell the difference between an **M** and a **W** in a design; therefore, please consider these patterns interchangeable. Two colors are needed for the letters with a third for the background. Sixteen mesh are needed in length for each letter, and twenty-one mesh are needed to turn the corner.

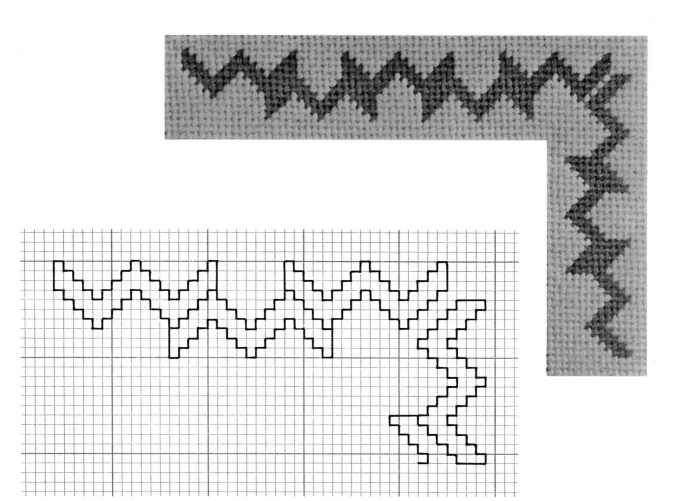

Just two colors are needed for the **X** pattern. It doesn't really matter if they are not of equal value. Find the center of the canvas and work one **X** right in the middle, then work out from there. This way your design will look evenly placed.

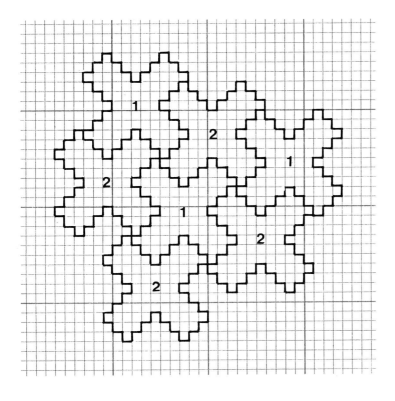

PATTERN 78

Five colors are needed for the **Y** pattern and their selection is a delicate one. The color you choose for the centers of the **Y**'s can be a relatively weak one, but the other four should be fairly well balanced against each other. Find the center of the canvas and work one **Y**. Work the rest of the canvas out from the center **Y**. This will ensure the pattern coming out evenly on all four sides.

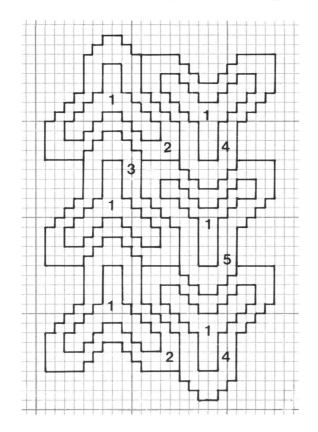

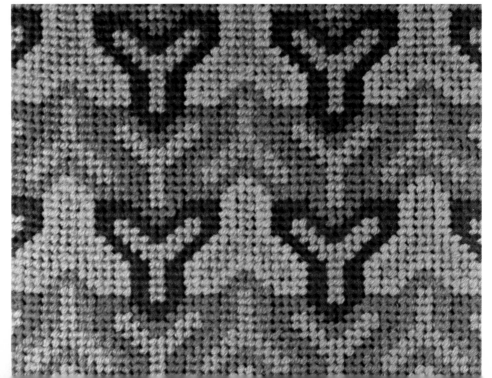

The letter **Z** has such a sharp, distinctive look there is little point in trying to disguise it. Only two colors are needed for this pattern. Since it is such a large motif, good strong colors should be used.

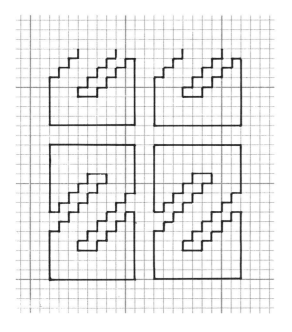

THREE VERSIONS OF THE HALF CROSS STITCH

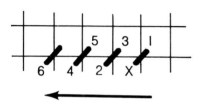

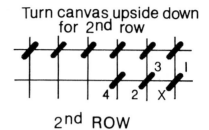

Turn canvas upside down for 2nd row

2nd ROW

THE CONTINENTAL STITCH

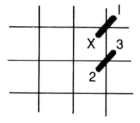

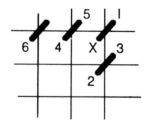

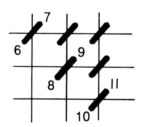

THE BASKET-WEAVE STITCH

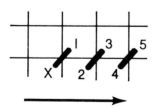

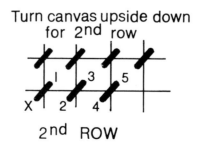

Turn canvas upside down for 2nd row

2nd ROW

QUICKPOINT

BRICK STITCH

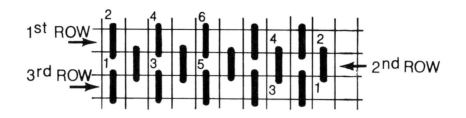

BARGELLO STITCH

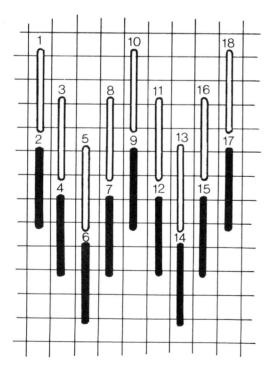

A SIMPLE BARGELLO PATTERN

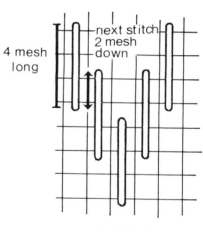

A 4/2 STEP

THE KALEM STITCH OR THE KNIT STITCH

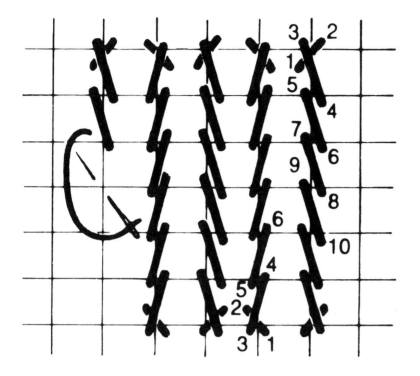

THE SMYRNA CROSS STITCH

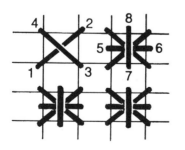

SCOTCH STITCH

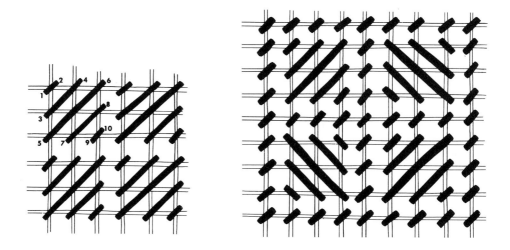

THE MOSAIC STITCH OR THE GERMAN STITCH

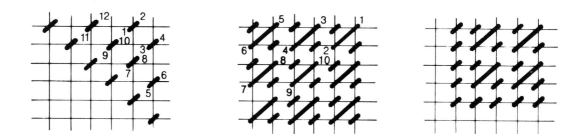

THE RUNNING CROSS STITCH OR THE LONG CROSS STITCH

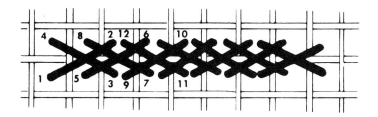

THE BYZANTINE STITCH

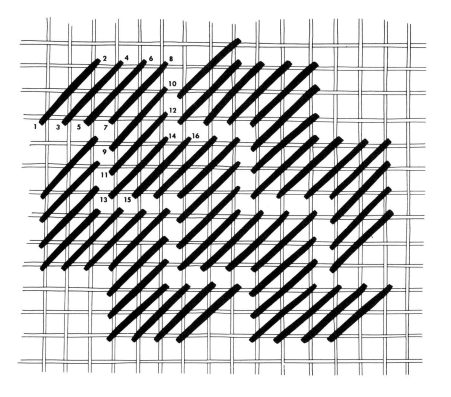

BIBLIOGRAPHY

Alexander, Mary Jane. *Handbook of Decorative Design and Ornament.* New York: Tudor Publishing Company, 1965.

Barrett, Cyril. *Op Art.* New York: The Viking Press, 1970.

Bradbee, Mrs. *The Ladies' Fancy Needle-Work Instructor.* London, 1842.

Chevreul, M. E. *The Principles of Harmony and Contrast of Colors and Their Applications to the Arts.* Introductory and Explanatory Notes by Faber Birreu. New York: Reinhold Publishing Company, 1967.

Christie, Archibald H. *Pattern Design, an Introduction to the Study of Formal Ornament.* New York, Dover Publishing Company, 1969.

Colby, Averil. *Samplers: Yesterday and Today.* London: B. T. Batsford, Ltd., 1964.

Emerson, Sybil. *Design, a Creative Approach.* Scranton: International Textbook Company, 1953.

Franses, Jack. *European and Oriental Rugs for Pleasure and Investment.* New York: Arco Publishing Company, 1970.

Gillon, Edmund V. *Geometric Design and Ornament.* New York: Dover Publications, 1969.

Hawley, Walter. *Oriental Rugs Antique and Modern.* New York: Dover Publications, 1970.

Huish, Marcus. *Samplers and Tapestry Embroideries.* New York: Dover Publications, 1970.

Humbert, Claude. *Ornamental Design.* New York: The Viking Press, Studio Book, 1970.

Justema, William. *The Pleasures of Pattern.* New York: Reinhold Publishing Company, 1968.

Kuhnel, Ernst. *The Minor Arts of Islam.* Translated by Katherine Watson. Ithaca, New York: Cornell University Press, 1971.

Lesiak, Sister Michaeline, O.S.F. *The Art of Fine Lettering: Basic Skill and Techniques.* Notre Dame, Indiana: University of Notre Dame Press, 1965.

Matthew, Sir Robert. *History of the House*. New York: G. P. Putnam Sons, 1971.

Mirow, George. *A Treasury of Design for Artists and Craftsmen*. New York: Dover Publications, 1969.

Parola, René. *Optical Art Theory and Practice*. New York: Beekman House, 1969.

Proctor, Richard M. *The Principles of Pattern for Craftsmen and Designers*. New York: Van Nostrand Reinhold Company, 1969.

Weeks, Jeanne G., and Treganowan, Donald. *Rugs and Carpets of Europe and the Western World*. Philadelphia: Chilton Book Company, 1969.

Yohe, Ralph S., and Jones, A. McCoy, eds. *Turkish Rugs*. The Washington Hajji Baba, Washington: The Textile Museum, 1968.

Magazine Article and Pamphlet

Crowfoot, Grace M., and Sutton, Phyllis M. "Ramallah Embroidery." *Embroidery*, vol. 3, no. 2 (March 1935), London.

Florence Home Needlework. Florence, Massachusetts: Nonotuck Silk Company, 1888.

NOTES